HAPPY TRAILS!

a National Parks journal

RP STUDIO
PHILADELPHIA

RP Studio™
Hachette Book Group
1290 Avenue of the Americas, New York, NY 10104
www.runningpress.com
@Running_Press

Printed in China

First Edition

Published by RP Studio, an imprint of Perseus Books, LLC, a subsidiary of Hachette Book Group, Inc. The RP Studio name and logo is a trademark of the Hachette Book Group.

The publisher is not responsible for websites (or their content) that are not owned by the publisher.

Text by Matt Garczynski

Design by Jenna McBride

ISBN: 978-0-7624-6899-7

1010

10 9 8 7 6 5 4 3 2 1

PARKS I'VE VISITED

NAME OF PARK	DATE

Yellowstone boasts more plentiful geysers than anywhere else on earth, thanks to the volcanic activity underfoot in the Yellowstone Caldera.

THE "DRY" IN "DRY TORTUGAS" COMES FROM THEIR LACK OF FRESH DRINKING WATER. THE PARK'S HISTORIC FORT JEFFERSON WAS BUILT WITH A SERIES OF RAINWATER CISTERNS IN ITS WALLS.

MANY OF THE PLACE NAMES IN ROCKY MOUNTAIN NATIONAL PARK COME FROM A 1914 EXPEDITION BY TWO ARAPAHO ELDERS, WHO RECALLED THE NATURAL LANDMARKS OF THEIR YOUTH.

The stony stumps and logs of Petrified Forest date back to when the northern Arizona desert was a flat subtropical plain.

CAPITOL REEF LIES ALONG THE WATERPOCKET FOLD, AN UPTHRUST CREST IN THE EARTH EXTENDING A HUNDRED MILES ACROSS THE UTAH DESERT.

MY FAVORITE PARKS

CARLSBAD CAVERNS WAS FORMED BY AN "ACID BATH" OF GROUND-WATER AND HYDROGEN SULFIDE, WHICH ATE AWAY AT THE UNDERGROUND LIMESTONE AS THE WATER TABLE DESCENDED.

The Paiute name for Zion is Mukuntuweap, meaning "Straight Canyon."

THE KIPAHULU DISTRICT OF HALEAKALĀ IS AN EXAMPLE OF AN *AHUPUA'A*, A TRADITIONAL LAND DIVISION SET UP TO PROTECT NATURAL RESOURCES.

A SEMI-REGULAR DOSE OF WILDFIRES ALLOWS THE MASSIVE
SEQUOIA TO RELEASE ITS SEEDS INTO THE SOIL.

PARKS I WANT TO VISIT

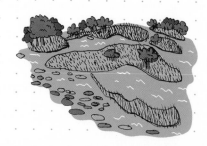

The Everglades' incredible bird populations were severely thinned during a turn-of-the-century craze for feathered hats.

THE NAMESAKE CACTUS OF SAGUARO NATIONAL PARK OFTEN GROWS TO BETWEEN 40 AND 60 FEET TALL, AND CAN THRIVE IN SCORCHING CONDITIONS FOR UP TO 200 YEARS.

THE CHANNEL ISLANDS HAVE BEEN CALLED "CALIFORNIA'S GALÁPAGOS" FOR THE ARCHIPELAGO'S MANY ENDEMIC SPECIES. THEY HAVE SAT ISOLATED FROM THE MAINLAND SINCE THEY WERE FORMED.

Acadia's diverse treescape was ensured by the Fire of 1947, which burned many of its old-growth evergreens and gave sun-loving species a chance to thrive.

THE INHABITANTS OF MESA VERDE LEFT AROUND 1300 CE, LEAVING
BEHIND COOKWARE, TOOLS, CLOTHING, AND 600 CLIFF DWELLINGS.

INDIANA DUNES ENJOYS SOME OF THE MOST DIVERSE PLANT LIFE IN ALL THE NATIONAL PARKS. YOU MIGHT FIND ARCTIC BEARBERRY GROWING BESIDE PRICKLY PEAR CACTUS.

The massive branches of redwood trees accrue deep organic soil mats, from which plants, shrubs, and even other full-size trees can grow.

MY IDEAL NATIONAL PARKS ROAD TRIP WOULD INCLUDE STOPS AT...

THE GREAT SMOKY MOUNTAINS ARE NAMED FOR THE HAZY MIST OFTEN SEEN RISING FROM THE TREETOPS.

THE CLEAR BLUE CRATER LAKE IS THE DEEPEST LAKE IN THE UNITED STATES, FORMED WHEN MOUNT MAZAMA ERUPTED AND COLLAPSED 7,700 YEARS AGO.

According to Paiute lore, the *hoodoos* of Bryce Canyon were once the ancient Legend People, who were turned to stone by Coyote for abusing the desert's resources.

THE PARKS I COULD VISIT OVER AND OVER AGAIN

LASSEN VOLCANIC NATIONAL PARK WAS ESTABLISHED IN 1916 TO PROTECT THE LANDSCAPE FORMED BY THE NEWLY ERUPTED LASSEN PEAK VOLCANO.

WIND CAVE IS NAMED FOR THE EERIE "BREATHING" EFFECT THAT OCCURS WHEN THE AIR PRESSURE BETWEEN THE MOUTH OF THE CAVE AND ITS INNER CHAMBERS VARIES.

The name *Black Canyon of the Gunnison* derives from the park's eerie black-stained walls, parts of which receive less than an hour's sunlight in a single day.

NINETY-FIVE PERCENT OF BISCAYNE NATIONAL PARK IS UNDERWATER.

AT A SPRAWLING 20,625 SQUARE MILES, ALASKA'S WRANGELL–
ST. ELIAS IS THE MOST MASSIVE NATIONAL PARK IN THE
UNITED STATES.

MY PERFECT DAY AT A PARK WOULD INCLUDE...

_____

_____

_____

_____

_____

_____

_____

_____

_____

_____

_____

_____

_____

_____

_____

_____

_____

_____

_____

_____

_____

_____

_____

In Olympic National Park's mossy rainforest, new trees can be seen taking root in old stumps and hollow logs.

BIG BEND IS NAMED FOR THE BROAD MEANDERING PATH CARVED BY
THE RIO GRANDE THROUGH THE CHIHUAHUAN DESERT.

ARCHES' LANDSCAPE ARCH IS CONSIDERED THE LONGEST NATURAL STONE SPAN IN NORTH AMERICA.

Voyageurs is named for the French-Canadian fur trappers who once paddled birch bark canoes through the waterways of Northern Minnesota.

AT THEIR CURRENT RATE OF EROSION, THE SANDSTONE BUTTES AND PINNACLES OF BADLANDS WILL BE AROUND FOR ONLY 500,000 MORE YEARS.

THE MOST SURPRISING THINGS I'VE SEEN IN NATIONAL PARKS